Recorder *from the* Beginn

AROUND THE WORLD

John Pitts

Around The World is an unique collection of songs and dances from around the world. The forty countries represented offer a wide variety of styles and rhythms, making the music both challenging and fun to perform by recorder players of any age.

In addition, the wide-ranging repertoire forms a useful multi-cultural resource, offering cross-curricular links with the many countries represented. Many of the items are also provided with some background information about the music and/or the country, or both. Where possible, suggestions are included for percussion accompaniments and rhythm ostinatos, usually in the Pupil's Book, but cross-referenced to the Teacher's Book when necessary.

The Pupil's Book also includes guitar chord symbols. The Teacher's Book includes the piano accompaniments for all the pieces, as well as the extra information listed above. Both books include a detailed cross-reference to all the other international music that is contained within the author's popular recorder teaching scheme.

Whilst ideal for players who have completed Book 1 of the *Recorder From The Beginning* tutor, *Around The World* can be used alongside all methods to provide additional repertoire and help promote stylistic awareness. All the items have been carefully arranged and graded, with the systematic increase in range of notes listed in the Contents page.

Chester Music Limited
(A division of Music Sales Limited)
8/9 Frith Street, London W1D 3JB

Contents

*Notes listed as "included" do not necessarily appear often in a piece.
  It is best to assess each item individually.

Acknowledgements:
Grateful thanks are due to the following for their kind help and assistance in finding suitable items for the book: Pat Dye, Music Section, British Library DSC, Boston Spa; Dharambir Singh, Lecturer in Indian Music, Leeds College of Music; Marcos Bednarski, Embassy of Argentine Republic; Marcelle Black, Leeds; Alan Tongue, Cambridge; Adele Pitts, Leeds.

This book © Copyright 2000 Chester Music.
Order No. CH61542 ISBN 0-7119-7690-2

Music processed by Stave Origination.
Cover design by Jon Forss.
Printed in the United Kingdom by Caligraving Limited, Thetford, Norfolk.

The Mountains of Mourne   Irish

The Pupil's Book includes
information about Mourne

Words and music by Percy French & H.Collison
Arr. John Pitts

La Jesucita   Mexican

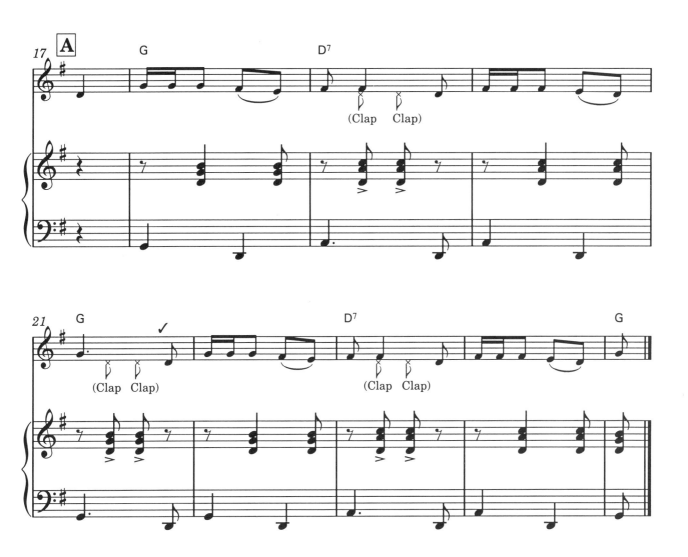

The Pupil's Book includes the following suggestions for rhythm accompaniments. They will enhance the piece, whether or not the piano is also used.

Ask some friends to play these rhythm ostinatos. From **A** they should clap instead, where shown in the music.

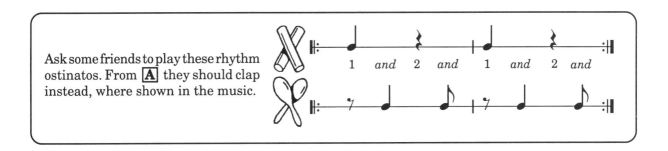

Do Di Li   Israeli

Come with me

The Pupil's Book includes suggestions for the clapping.

8

Bi Bi Og Blaka   Icelandic
Bye Bye and hushabye

This popular lullaby helps children fall asleep by describing swans flying by, and lambs playing on the hills.

9

Pentozalis   Greek

Cretan Dance Song

Fairly quick

Arirang   Korean

Information about the song is in the Pupil's Book.

NB. The Pupil's music is written out in full without the D.C. used here.

Viva Panama   Panamanian
Tamborito Dance

Information about the dance is in the Pupil's Book.

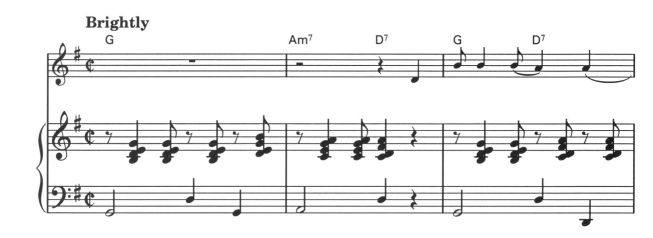

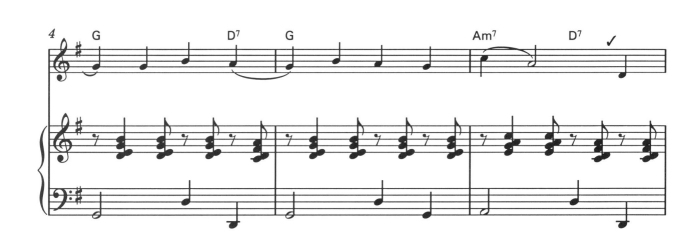

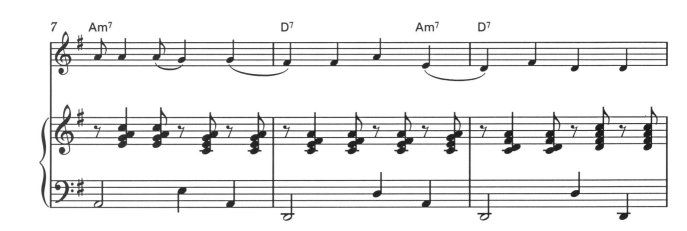

13

Tongo   Polynesian

Polynesia is a group of islands in the Pacific Ocean. It includes Hawaii, Samoa, Tonga, Cook Islands and Tahiti. Captain Cook visited several of the islands during his voyages in the 1770's.

Swing Low, Sweet Chariot   American Spiritual

Spirituals are the religious folksongs of America. Negro spirituals first arose among the black slave population and were often a song of religious hope for freedom. The music was influenced by the European hymns and harmonies introduced by the religious missionary movement.

Nans' Ingonyanma   South African Zulu
Here is the Lion

(Keep clapping on every beat)

Advice on the clapping is in the Pupil's Book.

An Eriskay Love Lilt   Hebridean

Information on Eriskay is in the Pupil's Book.

Words and music by Kenneth MacLeod and Marjory Kennedy-Fraser
Arr. John Pitts

20

Over The Sea To Skye Scottish

Kalinka   Russian

Teaching hint: teachers directing from the piano may need to use a dramatic nod of the head to signify when the pauses have been held long enough. A slow head-lift warns the players, and the downward nod indicates the first beat of the next bar.

Sur Le Pont D'Avignon   French

Information about the bridge is in the Pupil's Book.

Alouette French

Men Of Harlech   Welsh

Information about Harlech is in the Pupil's Book.

2 = optional alternative fingering. See Pupil Book page 47.

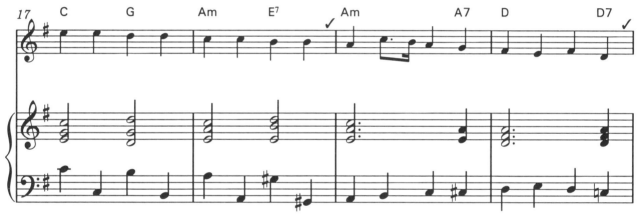

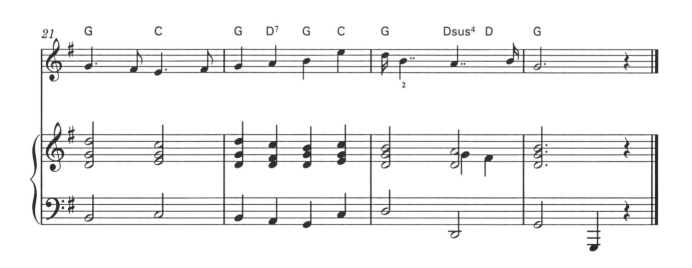

Mi Chacra   Spanish
My Ranch

Information about the song is in the Pupil's Book.

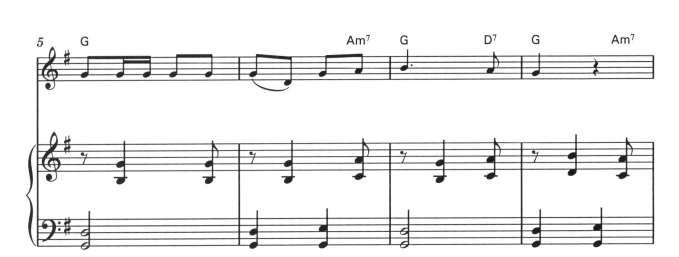

29

Guantanamera   Cuban

This tune is a folksong. The title means 'Girl from Guatanamo', a city in Cuba.

Lyric adaptation by Julian Orbon based on a poem by Jose Marti.
Music adaptation by Pete Seeger and Julian Orbon.
Arr. John Pitts.

Steady beguine

Percussion accompaniment.

The Pupil's Book gives these two rhythm patterns and advice on playing them.

1 (2) 3 4   1 (2) 3 4

1 *and* 2 *and* 3 *and* 4 *and*   1 *and* 2 *and* 3 *and* 4 *and*

Weggis Leid   Swiss Yodelling song

Sakura Japanese
Cherry Blossoms

Information about the song is in the Pupil's Book.

Pensively

El Tortillero   Chilean

The Tortilla Vendor

A tortilla (pronounced 'tor-tee-ya') is a thin pancake made from maize. They are often sold by street vendors.

With a steady swing ♩ = 156

34

Try adding some percussion to enhance the music; use claves, triangle and guiro.

Use this for the first section.

From [A] use this instead.

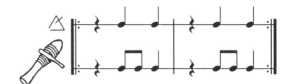

Chulu M'Chol Habora   Israeli

Dance the Hora

(shout - 'Hey!')

Waikaremoana   New Zealand - Maori

The 2nd Recorder part is optional. The song belongs to the Tuhoe people, who live near Lake Waikaremoana on New Zealand's North Island.

38

* For G♯ fingering see Pupil Book page 47.

O Waly Waly English

Scarborough Fair   English

Information about the tune is in the Pupil's Book.

41

Chula Portuguese

Dance Song

Mocirişă   Romanian

Oberek   Polish

Polonaise Polish

Information about the dance is in the Pupil's Book.

Rhythmic and stately

Bengali Folk Tune   Indian

The Pupil's Book includes information about Indian music, also some ostinatos to play.

46

Hua Ku Ko Chinese
Flower Drum Song

This song is described in the Pupil's Book.

Look Out, How It's Raining Austrian

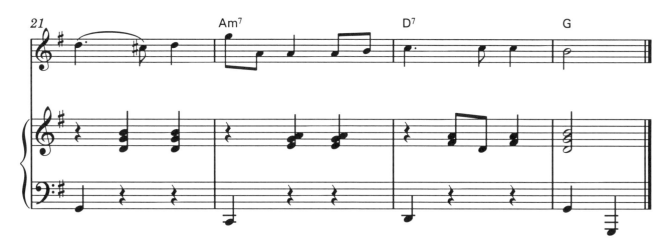

The Pupil's Book has some rhythm accompaniments to try.

This tune is a **waltz**, a dance in 3/4 time with usually only one harmony (chord) in each bar, as here. The bass part has the lowest note of the chord on the first beat, and the rest of the chord is on the other beats, giving an 'um-pah-pah' rhythm.

The waltz developed as a ballroom dance out of a peasant dance called the ländler which was popular in Austria and Germany. In the 1770's Mozart and others wrote many waltzes for the balls of Vienna. The dance swept through Europe during the first part of the nineteenth century, reaching the height of its development in the music of the Strauss family. At one time it was felt to be rather immoral because it was one of the first dances in which you held your partner close to you!

Not all waltzes are for dancing. The waltz rhythm was so popular that many composers wrote pieces just for concert performance, including the piano music of Chopin, Schumann and Brahms, the symphonies of Tchaikovsky and the orchestral music of Ravel.

The Austrian style 'Um-pah Band' (with the players dressed in 'lederhosen') is popular today, particularly at beer festivals!

By The Rivers Of Babylon   Jamaican

'By the Rivers of Babylon' is an old Rastafarian tune which has appeared in several different arrangements recorded by pop-groups. The words of the song are based on Psalm 137.

Reggae is the most famous kind of Jamaican music. A reggae song has four basic musical ingredients. The lowest is a short bass guitar tune, repeated over and over again and called a riff. There are two accompaniments to go with the riff. The first is a repeated percussion rhythm. The second accompaniment is played on guitar or organ. It consists of chords played firmly, on the second and fourth beats of the bar. Often the chords are played twice, quickly, to give a bouncy feeling. The fourth ingredient is the tune.

Zinga-za Samba Brazilian

The Pupil's Book includes information about the samba, also some ostinatos to play.

52

Stodola Pumpa   Czech

The Pupil's Book has percussion suggestions, using a tambourine for the A section and claves for the B section.

Nina Nana Italian
Lullaby

Santa Lucia   Italian

Not too fast

2 = optional alternative fingering. See Pupil Book page 47.

De Klokken   Belgian, Flemish
The Bells

The Ash Grove   English

Duerme Niño, Pequeñito Colombian

Sleep My Baby

Try using the beguine rhythms in the Pupil's Book page 19 to make an accompaniment.

Colombia is a country in South America, and has Brazil, Venezuela and Panama as next-door neighbours. There is music from all these countries in this book. Colombian folk music is a blend of Indian, Spanish and negro African elements.

Native instruments still in popular use include the *pan pipes,* various drums such as the *bomba,* and the notched gourd, the *guacharacas.*

Ola Glomstulen   Norwegian

This folksong tells the story of Ola Glomstulen, a miser who decided to get married.

La Cumparsita Uruguayan

G.H. Matos Rodriguez
arr. John Pitts

See Pupil's Book page 41 for some tango information and rhythms to play.

64

Chiapanecas   Mexican

Clapping Dance

The part for Recorder II is optional

66

Ask someone to clap in the chorus where shown in the music.

68

El Choclo Argentinian

The Pupil's Book includes some tango information and rhythms to play.

Angel Villoldo
Arr. John Pitts

Steady tango

70

Gaaer Jeg Udi Skoven   Danish

In Forest and Meadow

The Lorelei German

The Lorelei legend is described in the Pupil's Book.

El Lanero   Venezuelan

Cowboy dance

Ricardo Romero
Arr. John Pitts

shout-'O - le!'

Waltzing Matilda   (Australian)

Words by A.B. Patterson
Music by Mari Cowan
Arr. John Pitts

Index of Countries

Other International music in the series: *Recorder from the Beginning*